THE MERCHANT OF VENICE

by
William Shakespeare

Student Packet

Written by:
Gloria Levine, M. A.
Mary L. Dennis, Editor

Contains masters for:

- 2 Prereading Activities
- 1 Study Guide
- 4 Vocabulary Activities
- 3 Literary Analysis Activities
- 2 Critical Thinking Activities
- 3 Writing Activities
- 1 Crossword Puzzle (Review Activity)
- 2 Comprehension Quizzes (two levels)*
- 2 Unit Exams (two levels)*

PLUS Detailed Answer Key

Level II is more difficult than Level I.

Note
The text used to prepare this guide was the Signet Classic softcover published by the Penguin Group; Sylvan Barnet, General Editor. If other editions are used, scene and line numbers may vary.

ISBN 1-58130-567-2

© 1998 Novel Units, Inc. All rights reserved. Printed in the United States of America. Limited reproduction permission: The publisher grants permission to individual teachers who have purchased this book, or for whom it has been purchased, to reproduce the blackline masters as needed for use with their own students. Reproduction for an entire school or school district or for commercial use is prohibited.

To order, contact your local school supply store, or—

Novel Units, Inc.
P.O. Box 791610
San Antonio, TX 78279

Name_____

The Merchant of Venice
Activity #1 • Shakespeare's Language
Use Before Reading

Group activity
Shakespeare used many words that are now rare or obsolete—or now mean something else. When he couldn't quite find the word to suit his meaning, he frequently made one up! You don't need to understand the meaning of every single word or line that Shakespeare wrote. What matters is that you enjoy his wonderful—and often playful—use of language.

Before you study *The Merchant of Venice*, take a look at the following list of words from the play. Brainstorm possible definitions and use each word or phrase in a sentence. Have fun writing imaginative sentences—and later comparing your definitions with the actual ones.

Word (Act.scene.line)	Definition	Sentence
1. moe (1.1.108)		
2. dumbshow (1.2.72)		
3. eanlings (1.3.76)		
4. doit (1.3.137)		
5. martlet (2.9.27)		
6. forespurrer (2.9.94)		
7. knapped (3.1.9)		
8. shrowd (3.2.243)		
9. bankrout (4.1.122)		
10. tucket (5.1.121)		

© Novel Units, Inc.   All rights reserved

Name_____ *The Merchant of Venice*
Activity #2 • Journal Writing
Use Before Reading

Directions
Freewrite for a few minutes, using each of the following sentence-starters. Later, compare your responses with what you find in the play.

Act I
1. When a friend is down _____
_____

2. Borrowing money _____
_____

Act II
3. A good test of whether a man and woman are compatible _____
_____

4. A daughter might take money from her father without asking _____
_____

Act III
5. Revenge _____
_____

6. "A friend of his is a friend of mine" _____
_____

Act IV
7. Showing mercy _____
_____

8. Playing a trick on someone you love _____
_____

Act V
9. Relief is when _____
_____

10. All's well that ends well _____
_____

© Novel Units, Inc.   All rights reserved

Name_____   *The Merchant of Venice*
                                         Study Questions
                                         Use During Reading

Act I, Scene I
1. In the opening scene, what do Antonio's friends assume he is worried about?
2. In actuality, what is troubling Antonio?
3. What does Gratiano mean when he says, *"But...gudgeon"* (101-102)?
4. Why does Bassanio need money?
5. Why doesn't Antonio just give his friend the money?

Act I, Scene II
1. Why doesn't Portia feel she can simply choose the man she wishes to marry?
2. How is the choice among Portia's suitors to be made?
3. What does Portia have against the Neapolitan prince?
4. What does Portia have against Count Palatine?
5. What does Portia have against Monsieur Le Bon?
6. What does Portia have against Falconbridge?
7. What does Portia have against the Scottish lord?
8. What does Portia have against the young German?
9. Which suitor does Nerissa feel best deserves her lady?
10. How can you tell that Portia does not like the Prince of Morocco?

Act I, Scene III
1. How much does Bassanio borrow from Shylock?
2. What are the conditions of Shylock's loan?
3. What does Shylock mean when he says, *"Antonio is a good man"* (12)?
4. What is Shylock's response to Bassanio's dinner invitation?
5. Why does Shylock bring up Jacob and the sheep?
6. How has Antonio mistreated Shylock in the past—and why?

Name_____ *The Merchant of Venice*
Study Questions
page 2

7. Does Antonio promise to treat Shylock better in return for the loan?

8. Does Bassanio encourage Antonio to seal the bond with Shylock?

9. Why does Antonio say, *"The Hebrew will turn Christian"* (175)?

Prediction
Will Antonio forfeit on the debt?

Act II, Scene I
1. Where is this scene set?

2. Why does the Prince of Morocco offer to show Portia his blood?

3. What test did Portia's late father devise for her suitors?

Act II, Scene II
1. What dilemma does Launcelot face?

2. What does Launcelot's conscience tell him to do?

3. Why doesn't Launcelot's father recognize him?

4. What lie does Launcelot tell his father, at first?

5. What reason does Launcelot give for deciding to leave Shylock?

6. What present has Gobbo brought for Shylock?

7. Why does Gratiano want to accompany Antonio to Belmont?

Act II, Scene III
1. How does Jessica react to Launcelot's news that he is leaving?

2. What does Jessica give to Launcelot?

3. What does Jessica plan to do after she leaves her father?

4. What does Jessica mean when she says, *"…though I am a daughter to his blood, /I am not to his manners"* (18-19)?

Name_____ The Merchant of Venice
Study Questions
page 3

Act II, Scene IV
1. What invitation is Launcelot delivering to Shylock?

2. Why does Lorenzo give Launcelot some money?

3. Whom does Lorenzo arrange to meet at Gratiano's lodging?

4. What does Lorenzo reveal about the contents of Jessica's letter?

Act II, Scene V
1. Where is Shylock going?

2. According to Shylock, why has he accepted the invitation?

3. What does Shylock say to Launcelot about his new employer?

4. Why does Launcelot say, *"Your worship was wont to tell me I could do nothing without bidding"* (9)?

5. What instructions does Shylock give Jessica?

6. What is Jessica planning to do?

Act II, Scene VI
1. Who are Gratiano and Salerio waiting for?

2. How is Jessica disguised—and why?

3. What do Gratiano and Antonio talk about?

Act II, Scene VII
1. Why does Portia show the Prince of Morocco the three caskets?

2. What is the inscription on the gold casket?

3. What is the inscription on the silver casket?

4. What is the inscription on the lead casket?

5. Why does the Prince of Morocco choose the gold casket?

6. What does Morocco find in the gold casket?

© Novel Units, Inc.   All rights reserved

Name_____ *The Merchant of Venice*
Study Questions
page 4

Act II, Scene VIII
1. Why did Shylock have Bassanio's ship searched?
2. Why has Bassanio gone away on the ship?
3. Why are Solanio and Salerio planning to visit Antonio?

Act II, Scene IX
1. What do the suitors have to promise before they take the "test"?
2. Which casket does the Prince of Aragon choose—and why?
3. What news does the messenger bring?

Prediction
Which casket will Bassanio choose—and why?

Act III, Scene I
1. What bad news does Salerio bring?
2. How does Shylock react to his daughter's departure?
3. What does Shylock mean by, *"Let him look to his bond"*? (45)
4. Why does Shylock ask, *"Hath not a Jew eyes?"* (55)
5. What has Tubal been doing?
6. What has Jessica stolen from her father?
7. For what purpose does Shylock arrange to meet Tubal at the synagogue?

Act III, Scene II
1. Why does Portia suggest that Bassanio wait a day or two before choosing among the caskets?
2. Why does Portia give the order for music to be played?
3. Briefly, what is the song about?
4. Why doesn't Bassanio choose the gold casket?
5. Why does Bassanio choose the lead casket and what does he find inside?
6. According to Portia, what will happen if he loses the ring?

© Novel Units, Inc.   All rights reserved

Name_____

The Merchant of Venice
Study Questions
page 5

7. Why was Gratiano so eager for Bassanio to pick the right casket?

8. When Lorenzo shows up with Jessica, what does Gratiano call her?

9. What is in the letter Salerio brings Bassanio?

10. How does Portia react to the news about Antonio's loss?

11. What does Jessica tell the others about her father?

12. Why does Portia tell Bassanio to "be gone"?

Act III, Scene III

1. According to Antonio, why does Shylock refuse to show him mercy?

2. Why doesn't Antonio think the Duke will be able to help him?

Act III, Scene IV

1. Why is Portia sure that Antonio is worth helping?

2. What does Portia want Lorenzo to do while she is gone?

3. What does Portia tell Lorenzo she and Nerissa will be doing?

4. Who is Doctor Bellario?

5. What instructions does Portia give Balthasar?

6. What does Portia tell Nerissa about her plan?

Act III, Scene V

1. Why does Launcelot think that Nerissa is doomed?

2. How does Nerissa think her husband will "save" her?

3. Who is the father of "the Moor's" unborn baby?

4. What does Lorenzo want to talk about over dinner?

Prediction
Why is Portia disguising herself and Nerissa?

Act IV, Scene I

1. What is the Duke's opinion of Shylock?

2. What does the Duke mean when he tells Shylock, *"We all expect a gentle answer"*? (34)

© Novel Units, Inc.   All rights reserved

Name_____   *The Merchant of Venice*
Study Questions
page 6

3. What offer does Shylock turn down?

4. Why does Shylock mention pigs, cats, and bagpipes? (47-49)

5. Who are Nerissa and Portia pretending to be?

6. Who calls Shylock "harsh Jew" and "inexecrable dog"?

7. Why does Portia talk about mercy?

8. Why doesn't Shylock have a doctor standing by?

9. Does Antonio seem prepared to die or is he putting up a fight?

10. What do both Bassanio and Gratiano say they would give up to save Antonio?

11. How does Portia save Antonio?

12. What does Shylock lose as a result of the ruling?

13. How does the Duke show some mercy to Shylock?

14. What two requirements does Antonio add to Shylock's punishment?

15. What payment does (disguised) Portia request?

Act IV, Scene II

1. What is the deed Portia tells Nerissa to have Shylock sign?

2. How does Gratiano lose his ring?

Prediction
How will Gratiano and Bassanio explain the loss of their rings to their wives?

Act V, Scene I

1. What news do the messenger and Launcelot bring?

2. What do Portia and Nerissa hear, upon their return home?

3. What order does Portia have Nerissa give the servants?

4. Why do Nerissa and Gratiano start quarreling?

5. How do Gratiano and Bassanio explain the loss of their rings?

6. How do the two men get their rings back?

7. What additional good news does Portia have for Antonio?

8. What is the "manna" that Portia gives to Lorenzo and Nerissa?

Name_____   **The Merchant of Venice**
                                 Activity #3 • Shakespeare's Language
                                 Use After Reading (two pages)

I. Fill in the blanks, using words from the vocabulary box below. (Refer to the text of the play, if you need to.)

argosies	adieu	prolixity	bated	
shaft	patch	merchandise	amity	strange
surfeit	estimation	fancy	husbandry	balance
doublet	complexion	wanton	rasher	affections
rheum	presently	infidel	dram	amazed
livery	post	discharge	dam	

1. Mislike me not for my complexion,
   The shadowed _____ of the burnished sun. (2.1.2)

2. Your mind is tossing on the ocean,
   There where your _____ with portly sail— (1.1.9)

3. These griefs and losses have so _____ me
   That I shall hardly spare a pound of flesh
   Tomorrow to my bloody creditor (3.3.32)

4. But who comes here? Lorenzo and his _____! (3.2.218)

5. ...and yet for aught I see, they are as sick that _____ with too much
   as they that starve with nothing. (1.2.5-6)

6. This making of Christians will raise the price of hogs; if we grow all to be
   pork-eaters, we shall not shortly have a _____ on the coals for money.
   (3.5.24)

7. _____! (2.3.10) Tears exhibit my tongue. Most
   beautiful pagan, most sweet Jew, if a Christian do not play the knave and get thee,
   I am much deceived. But _____! (2.3.14)

8. You come to me and you say "Shylock, we would have moneys" — you say so,/
   You that did void your _____ upon my beard... (1.3.114)

© Novel Units, Inc.   All rights reserved

11

Name_____

The Merchant of Venice
Activity #3 • Shakespeare's Language
page 2

II. Match the words with their definitions using the vocabulary box on the previous page.

_____ 1. spittle

_____ 2. faithless one

_____ 3. uniform for a nobleman's retainers

_____ 4. good-bye; I commend you to God

_____ 5. slice of bacon

_____ 6. reduced; diminished

_____ 7. great merchant ships

_____ 8. are overfed

III. In the space below and on the back of this paper:
   a) Identify the speaker and the person addressed in each statement (see I, above).
   b) Paraphrase the statement (put the statement in your own words).
   c) Explain the context of the statement. (What caused the speaker to say this?)

_____
_____
_____
_____
_____
_____
_____
_____
_____
_____
_____
_____

Name_____ *The Merchant of Venice*
Activity #4 • Shakespeare's Language
Use After Reading

Shakespeare used many words which we use today—but in an UNFAMILIAR way. For example, when Launcelot hands Lorenzo the letter and says:
"And it shall please you to break up this," (2.4.10)
he means: "You'll want to open this."
NOT: "You'll want to smash this."

Circle the letter of the definition that BEST fits the **boldfaced** word in each sentence below. If Shakespeare used the word to mean what it most commonly means today, circle choice (d).

1. Go, draw aside the curtains and **discover**
   The several caskets to this noble Prince. (2.7.1)
   a) reveal   b) take   c) open   d) find out

2. The **villain** Jew with outcries raised the Duke,
   Who went with him to search Bassanio's ship. (2.8.4)
   a) dim-witted bachelor   b) faithless   c) low-bred fellow   d) rogue

3. Who chooseth me shall get as much as he **deserves**. (2.9.35)
   a) desires   b) risks   c) owes   d) merits

4. Thou hast contrived against the very life
   Of the defendant, and thou hast incurred
   The danger formerly by me **rehearsed**. (4.1.361)
   a) warned   b) cited   c) caused   d) practiced

5. Here in her hairs/The painter plays the spider, and hath woven/ A golden mesh t' entrap the hearts of men/**Faster** than gnats in cobwebs. (3.2.123)
   a) tighter   b) smaller   c) lighter   d) quicker

6. ....you shall find three of your argosies/Are richly come to harbor suddenly./ You shall not know by what **strange** accident/I chanced on this letter. (5.1.278)
   a) secret   b) astonishing   c) unfortunate   d) odd

7. The Duke himself, and the magnificoes/Of greatest port have all persuaded with him/ But none can drive him from the **envious** plea/ Of forfeiture, of justice, and his bond. (3.2.282)
   a) unrelenting   b) whining   c) malignant   d) jealous

© Novel Units, Inc.   All rights reserved

Name_____

The Merchant of Venice
Activity #5 • Shakespeare's Language
Use After Reading

Directions
Read the quotes and think about how someone today might express the same idea. Place the letter of the correct paraphrase in the blank. (For extra credit, create another "blooper"—wrong choice—on line c and give the resulting three-alternative quiz to a classmate.)

____ 1. If to do were as easy as to know what were good to do, chapels had been churches, and poor men's cottages princes' palaces. (1.2.12-14)
   a. It's a lot easier to know what you should do than it is to do it.
   b. A good pauper is worth a thousand ungodly princes in the eyes of the Church.
   c. _____

____ 2. When he is best, he is a little worse than a man; and when he is worst, he is little better than a beast. (1.2.86-88)
   a. He's a sorry excuse for a man even on his best day.
   b. When he is good he is very very good and when he is bad, he is horrid.
   c. _____

____ 3. The devil can cite Scripture for his purpose (1.3.95)
   a. The Bible explains why bad things sometimes happen to good people.
   b. He's so evil he can misuse the very Bible to support his actions.
   c. _____

____ 4. I am a Jew. Hath not a Jew eyes? Hath not a Jew hands, organs, dimensions, senses, affections, passions? (3.1.55-57)
   a. How can you ask me to deny my Jewishness?
   b. Isn't a Jew a human being like anyone else?
   c. _____

____ 5. There is no vice so simple but assumes
   Some mark of virtue in his outward parts. (3.2.82)
   a. Appearances can be deceiving; what you see is not always what you get—corruption can look like goodness.
   b. No one is all bad.
   c. _____

© Novel Units, Inc.   All rights reserved

Name_____

The Merchant of Venice
Activity #6 • Shakespeare's Language
Use After Reading

Directions
Shakespeare used certain words and phrases that were familiar to his listeners, but sound archaic and old-fashioned to us. Match each archaic term with its present-day "translation." Then include each archaic term in a sentence of your own, on the back of this paper. Try to sound as "Shakespearean" as you can!

___ 1. in sooth   a. dog, worthless person
___ 2. bechanced   b. to think, consider
___ 3. troth   c. for anything, whatever
___ 4. for aught   d. in the meantime
___ 5. afeard   e. it seemed to me
___ 6. whiles   f. hasten
___ 7. hath   g. in truth
___ 8. bethink me   h. faith
___ 9. albeit   i. rascal, scoundrel
___ 10. ye   j. although, even if
___ 11. methoughts   k. befell, happened
___ 12. goodly   l. immediately
___ 13. rheum   m. afraid
___ 14. cur   n. discharge, mucus, spit
___ 15. forthwith   o. of substantial size
___ 16. knave   p. has
___ 17. hie   q. you

© Novel Units, Inc.   All rights reserved

Name_____   ***The Merchant of Venice***
Activity #7 • Critical Thinking/Creative Writing
Use After Reading

Project
You are Portia. Before your father died, he cooked up a "test" your boyfriends had to take in order to decide which would marry you. There's only one you have any desire to marry, though. Write to an advice columnist for advice.

Step 1. Brainstorm the pros and cons of your father's plan and list them.
Step 2. Finish the letter you have started, below—using some of the ideas from Step 1.

Dear Gabby,
I have read your column for years, but I never thought that I would be writing to you. Before he died, my father_____
_____. Now, I loved my father and I certainly want to respect his wishes,_____
_____. His "test" has certain good points:_____. Also,
_____. On the other hand,
_____. The main problem I have is _____
_____. I've considered_____
_____. Or I could_____
_____. I could even_____
_____. What's your take on all of this?

Brooding in Belmont,

_____

Step 3. In small groups, brainstorm possible actions Portia might take—and weigh the pros and cons of each. (A chart for organizing your ideas is shown below.) Then write a letter of advice to Portia, using details from the completed chart.

Choice #1	Choice #2	Choice #3
pros cons	pros cons	pros cons

© Novel Units, Inc.   All rights reserved

Name_____

The Merchant of Venice
Activity #8 • Language Study: Malapropisms
Use During/After Reading

Malapropisms

A **malapropism** is the mistaken substitution of one word for another word that sounds similar.

Sample: 2.2.27   *"Certainly the Jew is the very devil incarnation."*
(Launcelot means "incarnate" here.)

A. Look up the derivation of "Malapropism." Who was Mrs. Malaprop?

B. Like the clownish figures in other Shakespearean comedies (e.g., Grumio in *Taming of the Shrew* and Dogberry in *Much Ado About Nothing*) Launcelot and Gobbo utter quite a few malapropisms.
For each of the mangled phrases in italics produced by Launcelot or Gobbo, below, write the word or phrase you think he meant.

1. 2.2.124, Gobbo: He hath a great infection,(_____) sir, as one would say, to serve—

2. 2.2.133, Launcelot: ...the Jew, having done me wrong, doth cause me, as my father, being I hope an old man, shall frutify (_____) unto you—

3. 2.2.136, Launcelot: ...the suit is impertinent (_____) to myself, as your worship shall know by this honest old man...

4. 2.2.142, Gobbo: That is the very defect (_____) of the matter, sir.

5. 2.3.10, Launcelot: Tears exhibit (_____) my tongue.

6. 2.5.20, Launcelot: My young master doth expect your reproach (_____.)

7. 3.5.4, Launcelot: I was always plain with you, and so now I speak my agitation (_____) of the matter.

C. On the back of your paper, list characters from TV, literature, etc. who are known for their malapropisms.

© Novel Units, Inc.   All rights reserved

Name_____

The Merchant of Venice
Activity #9 • Language Study: Puns
Use During/After Reading

Puns

A **pun** is an intentional play on words based on the similarity of sound between two words with different meanings: "They went and told the sexton and the sexton tolled the bell."

  A. For each pun, below, identify the speaker and explain the boldfaced word's two meanings.
   1. O my Antonio, I do know of these
      That therefore only are reputed wise
      For saying nothing; when I am very sure
      If they should speak, would almost dam those ears,
      Which hearing them would call their brothers fools. (1.1.99)

      Speaker:_____ a)_____ b)_____

   2. When he is **best** he is a little worse than a man, and when he is worst he is little better than a beast. (1.2.87-88)

      Speaker:_____ a)_____ b)_____

   3. Tell **gentle** Jessica I will not fail her. (2.4.19)

      Speaker:_____ a)_____ b)_____

   4. What, must I hold a candle to my shames?
      They in themselves, good sooth, are too too **light**. (2.6.42)

      Speaker:_____ a)_____ b)_____

   5. (In response to Gratiano's comment that "We are the Jasons, we have won the Fleece) I would you had won the **fleece** that he hath lost. (3.2.242)

  B. Use one of the pairs to write a pun that one of the speakers, above, might have made up.
     _____

  C. On the back of your paper. make a list of people you have met (in movies, books, real life, etc.) who enjoy punning.

© Novel Units, Inc.   All rights reserved

Name_____

The Merchant of Venice
Activity #10 • Literary Analysis
Use After Reading

Project: Allusions

An **allusion** is a figure of speech that makes brief reference to an historical or literary person or event. Shakespeare used several allusions to myths. He used them to create mood, reveal character, and emphasize the ironies in various situations.

Most audience members in Shakespeare's day were familiar with these references; the allusions were effective because there was a common body of knowledge shared by the writer and his audience members. However, readers today may need to do some research (using a dictionary, encyclopedia, biblical concordance, notes at the end of the play, etc.) to understand and appreciate these allusions.

1. Divide the list of allusions below among the group.
2. Write a paragraph explaining exactly to what the allusion(s) on your list refer. (Tell who, what, and when.) Cite your source(s).
3. Reread the entire section in which the allusion occurs, and write a paragraph about why Shakespeare used the allusion. (Tell what effect the allusion has on the reader's understanding of the situation, the character, the mood, etc.)
4. Write two allusions of your own. (For example, to what Shakespearean or biblical figure might you compare your best friend?)
5. Share your findings and allusions with the whole group.

Allusions in *The Merchant of Venice*:

    a. Phoebus (2.1.5)
    b. Hercules, Lichas, Alcides (2.1.32,35)
    c. Hagar (2.5.43)
    d. Troy, Dardanian wives (3.2.56,58)
    e. Jasons (3.2.241)
    f. Scylla and Charybdis (3.5.15-16)
    g. Daniel (4.1.222)
    h. Barabbas (4.1.295)
    i. Troilus and Cressid (5.1.4,6)
    j. Thisbe (5.1.7)
    k. Dido (5.1.10)
    l. Medea and Aeson (5.1.13-14)

© Novel Units, Inc.   All rights reserved

Name_____   *The Merchant of Venice*
Activity #11 • Writing to Inform and Convince
Use During/After Viewing (two pages)

Project
Write a movie review of the 1973 Jonathan Miller production of *The Merchant of Venice*, with Laurence Olivier, Jeremy Brett and Joan Plowright. Different actors and actresses have given differing interpretations to the roles of Shylock, Bassanio, Portia, and others in *The Merchant of Venice*.

I. Fill in this chart as you watch the movie—or right afterward. Briefly note what happens in each scene. What did the scene also show about the characters' "inner selves"—thoughts, feelings, motivations, personality?

Scene	What Happens	Inner Selves
1. Bassanio asks Antonio for money.		
2. Bassanio approaches Shylock about a loan.		
3. Shylock calls for Jessica before going to dinner at Bassanio's.		
4. Jessica leaves her father's house in disguise.		
5. Shylock learns that Jessica is gone and Antonio's ships lost.		
6. Shylock gets news of Jessica from Tubal.		
7. Bassanio and Portia both learn of Antonio's loss.		

© Novel Units, Inc.   All rights reserved

Name_____   *The Merchant of Venice*
                                      Activity #11 • page 2

Scene	What Happens	Inner Selves
8. The Duke makes his appeal to Shylock.		
9. Shylock demands his due.		
10. Portia, in disguise, wins the case for Antonio.		
11. Gratiano and Bassanio lose their rings.		
12. Lorenzo and Jessica declare their love for each other.		
13. Portia and Nerissa tease their husbands about the rings.		
14. Jessica learns that she will inherit her father's property upon his death.		

II. Write a review of the movie. Include these elements:
- Description of Joan Plowright's Portia
- Description of Laurence Olivier's Shylock
- How their Portia and Shylock resemble or differ from other versions—or Shakespeare's
- Most telling scenes
- Changes in Shakespeare's story—such as omission of Old Gobbo
- Comment on how well the 19th century setting "works."
- Comment on the setting, props, scenery, lighting, costuming, voices, gestures.
- How does the humor come across?
- What is Shakespeare saying about commitment—and Jewishness?

© Novel Units, Inc.   All rights reserved

Name_____ *The Merchant of Venice*
Activity #12 • Expository Writing
Use After Reading

Project
Write an essay in which you respond to *The Merchant of Venice* by exploring a problem posed by the play. The topic you choose should be something you think is important to discuss in order to understand the meaning of Shakespeare's work—and it should be something that you really wondered about as you reflected on the play.

1. Brainstorm a list of questions *The Merchant of Venice* raises in your mind. (Sample questions: Why did the author choose this title rather than, say "Shylock"? Why was Shylock so upset about Jessica's leaving? When is it "OK" to break a commitment?)
2. Choose the question you wonder about most.
3. Generate a possible answer to the question.
4. Write down some more questions this answer raises.
5. Write down a second possible answer to the initial question—or to the second question.
6. Continue in this way until you have written as many questions and answers as you can.
7. Read over what you have written and underline the idea that you find most intriguing.
8. Use this as the thesis statement for a five-paragraph essay about *The Merchant of Venice*.

   Paragraph 1: Introduce your thesis.
   Paragraph 2: Provide one example or reason in support of your thesis.
   Paragraph 3: Provide a second piece of supportive evidence.
   Paragraph 4: Provide a third piece of evidence.
   Paragraph 5: Summarize and emphasize your thesis.

9. Read your essay to other students and ask them for questions your writing raises in their minds.
10. Revise your essay in light of some of these questions.

Name_____

The Merchant of Venice
Activity #13 • Crossword Puzzle
Use After Reading

Across
1. Suitor to Portia
3. A Jew
4. Shylock's profession
7. This is heard while Bassanio comments on the caskets.
8. "Some men there are love not a gaping _____."
9. A. K. A. Portia
13. Country in which Merchant of Venice is set.
15. "Who chooseth the _____ casket must give and hazard all he hath."
17. "Hath not a _____ eyes?"

Down
2. "Who chooseth the _____ casket shall get as much as he deserves."
5. Bassanio and Gratiano give theirs away.
6. Shylock demands a pound of Antonio's _____.
7. Jessica trades Leah's ring for one of these.
8. Heiress loved by Bassanio
10. He is in love with Jessica.
11. Half of Shylock's wealth is forfeited to the _____.
12. Portia's estate
14. The winning casket
16. The winning casket contains Portia's _____.
17. Shylock's daughter
18. The bond gives Shylock no jot of _____.
21. Portia disguises herself as a doctor of _____.
22. Shylock's friend
23. Antonio borrows 3,000 of these.
24. He chooses the silver casket.

19. He pardons Shylock's life.
20. A clown; Shylock's servant
25. "Who chooseth the _____ casket shall gain what many men desire."
26. Shylock must become one.
27. Nerissa dresses as a lawyer's ___.
28. _____ of Shylock's fortune will eventually go to Lorenzo and Jessica.
29. Portia's maid

© Novel Units, Inc.

23

All rights reserved

Name_____   **The Merchant of Venice**
　　　　　　　　　　　　　　　　　　　Comprehension Quiz • Level I
　　　　　　　　　　　　　　　　　　　Use After Reading Acts I and II

True/False: Label the true statements T and the false statements F.

___ 1. Bassanio wants to rid himself of his debts and marry Portia.
___ 2. Antonio offers to give Bassanio three of his ships.
___ 3. Portia devised the coffer test because she wants to avoid marriage.
___ 4. The suitor who chooses the proper coffer wins Portia.
___ 5. Nerissa warns Portia that Bassanio is too poor for her.
___ 6. Shylock agrees to lend Bassanio 3000 ducats for three months.
___ 7. Shylock hates Bassanio, who has spat on him in the past.
___ 8. Antonio agrees to give a pound of flesh if the loan is forfeited.
___ 9. Shylock tells Jessica not to stay out too late with the masquers.
___ 10. Bassanio urges Antonio to accept Shylock's "pound of flesh" clause.
___ 11. Portia lives at Belmont, a lavish estate.
___ 12. Launcelot the Clown decides to leave his master, Shylock.
___ 13. Gobbo pretends not to recognize his son, Launcelot.
___ 14. Antonio hires Launcelot.
___ 15. Lorenzo promises Jessica he will convert to Judaism.

Matching: Match each effect with the statement that BEST describes the cause. Place the letter of the cause in the appropriate blank.

EFFECT

___ 16. Gratiano asks if he can accompany Bassanio to Belmont
___ 17. Jessica has Launcelot deliver a letter secretly
___ 18. Jessica takes gold and jewels from her father
___ 19. The Prince of Morocco knows he has not won Portia
___ 20. Shylock goes to search Bassanio's ship

CAUSE (because...)

a. he is looking for his missing daughter
b. he wants to keep his friend out of trouble
c. he is in love with Nerissa
d. she doesn't want her father to know she is running away
e. he finds a mirror inside the lead casket
f. she wants to go on a shopping spree as a newlywed
g. she wants to get back at him for always being so stingy toward her
h. he finds a death's head inside the gold casket

© Novel Units, Inc.　　　　　　　　　　All rights reserved

Name_____

The Merchant of Venice
Comprehension Quiz • Level II
Use After Reading Acts I and II

Fill-Ins
Below is a summary of the first act of *The Merchant of Venice*. Fill in each blank with the correct word, phrase, or name.

Scene I: In the opening scene, Antonio's mood is one of 1._____ . His friend Bassanio tells him that he is happy to announce that he is 2._____ and, as a result, wants to get rid of his 3._____. Antonio replies that all of his fortunes are with his 4._____, but he is willing to put up credit for his friend.

Scene II: Portia tells her 5._____ that she is feeling down. She is not happy about the "test" that her late 6._____ devised for her suitors. The one who chooses the 7._____ (gold, silver, or lead) with the right saying, wins Portia. Portia is not interested in any of the suitors. Nerissa says that 8._____, on the other hand, is worthy of her lady, and Portia happily agrees.

Scene III: Bassanio, meanwhile, approaches Shylock, the Jewish usurer, about a loan. Shylock agrees to lend 9._____ducats to Bassanio for 10._____ months, with Antonio bound. Shylock hates Antonio, who has, in the past, 11._____—in contrast with Shylock's money-lending practices. Antonio admits that, in the past, he has also 12._____ Shylock's clothes and spurned the Jewish people—and would do it again. Seemingly as a joke, Shylock adds a stipulation to the agreement: if he is not repaid on the given day, he will get 13._____; Antonio agrees to sign the bond, over 14._____'s protestations.

Short Answer
On the back of your paper, answer each question in one or two complete sentences.

15. After much soul-searching, what decision has Launcelot reached?

16. Who doesn't recognize Launcelot—and why?

17. Why is Jessica going to convert to Christianity?

18. What is in the letter that Jessica has Launcelot deliver?

19. What does Jessica take from her father—and why?

20. How does Shylock react when he learns that Jessica is gone?

© Novel Units, Inc.　　　　　　　　　　　　　　　　　　　　　　　　　　　　All rights reserved

Name_____   **The Merchant of Venice**
                                       Unit Test • Level I
                                       Objective Test

Identification
Write the letter of the character next to the correct description.

____	1. Antonio's friend, suitor to Portia	A. Antonio
____	2. Friends of Antonio and Bassanio	B. Bassanio
____	3. Blind old father of Launcelot	C. Gratiano
____	4. Jewish moneylender	D. Salerio and Solanio
____	5. In love with Jessica	E. Prince of Morocco
____	6. Dark-skinned suitor	F. Prince of Aragon
____	7. Servant to Bassanio	G. Lorenzo
____	8. Portia's waiting woman	H. Shylock
____	9. Wealthy heiress, in love with Bassanio	I. Tubal
____	10. Merchant; signs a bond for his friend, Bassanio	J. Launcelot
____	11. A Jew, Shylock's friend	K. Old Gobbo
____	12. Shylock's daughter; converts to Christianity	L. Leonardo
____	13. Clown, servant to Shylock	M. Portia
____	14. Suitor who chooses the silver casket, assuming he deserves Portia.	N. Nerissa
____	15. Quick-witted friend of Bassanio's, in love with Nerissa	O. Jessica

Sequence
Indicate the order in which the following events occurred in the play. Write the letters of the events in order next to the proper numbers. (The letter of the chronologically first event goes next to 16.)

____ 16.   a. Shylock insists on his pound of flesh.
____ 17.   b. Bassanio picks the lead coffer.
____ 18.   c. Shylock agrees to lend Antonio 3,000 ducats.
____ 19.   d. Portia gives her "quality of mercy" speech.
____ 20.   e. Shylock learns that Jessica has run off.

Quotations
For each quote, write the letter of the speaker next to the number.

____ 21. I hold the world but as the world, Gratiano, —
   A stage, where every man must play a part;
   And mine a sad one. (1.1.77-79)
   a) Shylock   b) Salerio   c) Bassanio   d) Antonio

© Novel Units, Inc.   All rights reserved

Name_____   *The Merchant of Venice*
　　　　　　　　　　　　　　　　　Unit Test • Level I
　　　　　　　　　　　　　　　　　page 2

____ 22. Fish not, with this melancholy bait,
For this fool gudgeon, this opinion. (1.1.101-102)
a) Antonio   b) Portia   c) Gratiano   d) Bassanio

____ 23. In my school-days, when I had lost one shaft,
I shot his fellow of the selfsame flight
The selfsame way, with more advised watch,
To find the other forth, and by adventuring both,
I oft found both. (1.1.140-145)
a) Bassanio   b) Antonio   c) Gratiano   d) Shylock

____ 24. They are as sick that surfeit with too much, as they that starve with nothing (1.2.5-6)
a) Nerissa   b) Portia   c) Shylock   d) Antonio

____ 25. The brain may devise laws for the blood, but a hot temper leaps o'er a cold decree. (1.2.17-19)
a) Shylock   b) Portia   c) Jessica   d) Lorenzo

____ 26. But ships are but boards, sailors but men: there be land-rats and water-rats, water-thieves and land-thieves. (1.3.21-23)
a) Gratiano   b) Shylock   c) Portia   d) Launcelot

____ 27. I will buy with you, sell with you, talk with you, walk with you, and so following; but I will not eat with you, drink with you, nor pray with you. What news on the Rialto? (1.3.33-36)
a) Antonio   b) Bassanio   c) Launcelot   d) Shylock

____ 28. The devil can cite Scripture for his purpose (1.3.95)
a) Portia   b) Shylock   c) Antonio   d) Bassanio

____ 29. You call me misbeliever, cut-throat dog,
And spet upon my Jewish gaberdine. (1.3.108-109)
a) Jessica   b) Shylock   c) Launcelot   d) Old Gobbo

____ 30. It is a wise father that knows his own child. (2.2.76-77)
a) Jessica   b) Shylock   c) Launcelot   d) Old Gobbo

____ 31. All that glisters is not gold
Often have you heard that told. (2.7.65-66)
These words were found on the scroll in the
a) lead chest   b) brass chest   c) silver chest   d) gold chest

© Novel Units, Inc.　　　　All rights reserved

Name_____   *The Merchant of Venice*
                                       Unit Test • Level I
                                       page 3

____ 32. I am a Jew. Hath not a Jew eyes? Hath not a Jew hands, organs, dimensions, senses, affections, passions? (3.1.55-57)
    a) Tubal   b) Shylock   c) Jessica   d) Launcelot

____ 33. There is no vice so simple but assumes
Some mark of virtue in his outward parts. (3.2.81-82)
    a) Shylock   b) Portia   c) Antonio   d) Bassanio

____ 34. The quality of mercy is not strain'd,
It droppeth as the gentle rain from heaven...
And that same prayer doth teach us all to render
The deeds of mercy. (4.1.183...201)
    a) Portia   b) Shylock   c) Antonio   d) Nerissa

____ 35. You take my house when you do take the prop
That doth sustain my house; you take my life
When you do take the means whereby I live. (4.1.374-376)
    a) Antonio   b) Bassanio   c) Shylock   d) Launcelot

Multiple Choice
To the left of each item number, write the letter of the BEST response

____ 36. *The Merchant of Venice* is classified as one of Shakespeare's
    A. tragedies
    B. comedies
    C. histories
    D. allegories

____ 37. Which of the following losses does NOT occur in *The Merchant of Venice*?
    A. loss of jewels
    B. loss of a daughter
    C. loss of a pound of flesh
    D. loss of merchant ships

____ 38. Which of the following does NOT describe Antonio?
    A. in love with an unnamed woman
    B. unapologetic to Shylock
    C. loyal to Bassanio
    D. mirthless and duty-bound

© Novel Units, Inc.   All rights reserved

Name_____   *The Merchant of Venice*
                                 Unit Test • Level I
                                 page 4

____ 39. Shylock, Bassanio, and Gratiano all lose _____ that had belonged to women close to them—and these _____ are all used as payment.
   A. pictures
   B. books
   C. letters
   D. rings

____ 40. Like Portia, Jessica
   A. is willing to give up her religion
   B. is in love with Bassanio
   C. is Jewish
   D. disguises herself as a male

____ 41. Portia honors her father by putting her suitors to the test devised by him; in contrast, Jessica
   A. insults her father and tells him she wishes she weren't Jewish
   B. steals from her father and elopes with a Christian
   C. talks back to her father and devises her own courtship test
   D. betrays her father by arranging for his arrest on charges of usury

____ 42. The most famous quote in *The Merchant of Venice* is probably
   A. "Hath not a Jew eyes?"
   B. "Out, out, damn spot!"
   C. "To be or not to be, that is the question."
   D. "Much ado about nothing!"

____ 43. Shylock's feelings toward Antonio are most similar to
   A. Cinderella's wicked step-sisters toward her
   B. Abel's feelings toward his brother Cain
   C. Hamlet's feelings toward his father's ghost
   D. Captain Ahab's feelings toward Moby Dick

____ 44. Portia is shopping for a small gift that will remind Bassanio of her. She would most likely buy him
   A. a bumper sticker that says, "Revenge is sweet."
   B. a card that says, "Finders keepers, losers weepers."
   C. a mug that says, "To err is human, to forgive—divine."
   D. a poster that says, "Don't look a gift horse in the mouth!"

Name_____

The Merchant of Venice
Unit Test • Level I
page 5

____ 45. At a nightclub, Gratiano would most likely be found
   A. sweating over the dishwasher in the kitchen
   B. drinking by himself in a dark corner
   C. onstage, performing a comedy routine
   D. playing melancholy strains on his saxophone

____ 46. Jessica and Shylock both convert to Christianity,
   A. but only Jessica seems happy about it
   B. and both do so because they are forced to
   C. but only Jessica does so because she hates being spat upon
   D. but only Shylock was actually Jewish

____ 47. Shylock demands his pound of flesh from Antonio even though Portia has offered
   A. to give a pound of her own flesh
   B. to repay the debt more than twice over
   C. to give him a high-paying job at Belmont
   D. to return his daughter if he forgives the debt

____ 48. In Shakespeare's day, the only job a Jewish person could legally hold was Shylock's—that of _____
   A. innkeeper
   B. clothier
   C. jeweler
   D. moneylender

____ 49. Shylock never gets his pound of flesh because it would have been illegal for—
   A. a moneylender to demand interest on his loan
   B. anyone to take flesh in return for a bad debt
   C. any Jewish alien to harm the life of a citizen
   D. a Jew to do business with a Christian

____ 50. Because Antonio and the Duke show Shylock some mercy, his life is spared and
   A. Jessica is ordered to repay half the amount she took from her father
   B. after his death half of his fortune goes to Lorenzo and Jessica
   C. Antonio promises to repay half of the debt
   D. he is allowed to become a Christian if he wants to

© Novel Units, Inc.   All rights reserved

Name_____   *The Merchant of Venice*
                                       Unit Test • Level II
                                       Written Response

Identification
Fill in the blanks with the names of the characters described.

_____ 1. Antonio's friend, suitor to Portia

_____ 2. Friends of Antonio and Bassanio

_____ 3. Blind old father of Launcelot

_____ 4. Jewish moneylender

_____ 5. In love with Jessica

_____ 6. Dark-skinned suitor

_____ 7. Servant to Bassanio

_____ 8. Portia's waiting woman

_____ 9. Wealthy heiress, in love with Bassanio

_____ 10. Merchant; signs a bond for his friend, Bassanio

_____ 11. A Jew, Shylock's friend

_____ 12. Shylock's daughter; converts to Christianity

_____ 13. Clown, servant to Shylock

_____ 14. Suitor who chooses silver, assuming he deserves Portia

_____ 15. Quick-witted friend of Bassanio's, in love with Nerissa

Vocabulary
Write a synonym or brief definition of each italicized word.

16. You that did void your *rheum* upon my beard... (1.3.114)

17. A quarrel, ho, already! What's the matter?
    About a hoop of gold, a *paltry* ring
    That she did give me...(5.1.147)
:

© Novel Units, Inc.   All rights reserved
                    31

Name_____

The Merchant of Venice
Unit Test • Level II
page 2

18. "Who chooseth me shall get as much as he deserves."/And well said, too, for who shall go about/To *cozen* fortune, and be honorable/ Without the stamp of merit? (2.9.37)

19. Your mind is tossing on the ocean/ There where your *argosies* with portly sail— (1.1.9)

20. Many times and oft/In the Rialto you have *rated* me (1.3.104)

Quotations
For each quote, below, tell who is speaking—and put the quote in your own words.

21. I hold the world but as the world, Gratiano—
A stage, where every man must play a part;
And mine a sad one. (1.1.77-79)

_____: _____
_____

22. Fish not, with this melancholy bait,
For this fool gudgeon, this opinion. (1.1.101-102)

_____: _____
_____

Name_____

The Merchant of Venice
Unit Test • Level II
page 3

23. In my school-days, when I had lost one shaft,
I shot his fellow of the selfsame flight
The selfsame way, with more advised watch,
To find the other forth, and by adventuring both,
I oft found both. (1.1.140-144)

_____ : _____
_____

24. They are as sick that surfeit with too much, as they that starve with nothing (1.2.5-6)

_____ : _____
_____

25. The brain may devise laws for the blood, but a hot temper leaps o'er a cold decree. (1.2.17-19)

_____ : _____
_____

26. But ships are but boards, sailors but men: there be land rats and water rats, water thieves and land thieves. (1.3.21-23)

_____ : _____
_____

27. I will buy with you, sell with you, talk with you, walk with you, and so following; but I will not eat with you, drink with you, nor pray with you. What news on the Rialto?
(1.3.33-36)

_____ : _____
_____

© Novel Units, Inc.   All rights reserved

Name_____

The Merchant of Venice
Unit Test • Level II
page 4

28. The devil can cite Scripture for his purpose. (1.3.95)

   _____ : _____
   _____

29. You call me misbeliever, cut-throat dog,
    And spit upon my Jewish gaberdine.(1.3.108-109)

   _____ : _____
   _____

30. It is a wise father that knows his own child. (2.2.76-77)

   _____ : _____
   _____

31. "All that glisters is not gold." (2.7.65)

   _____ : _____
   _____

32. I am a Jew. Hath not a Jew eyes? Hath not a Jew hands, organs, dimensions, senses, affections, passions? (3.1.55-57)

   _____ : _____
   _____

33. There is no vice so simple but assumes
    Some mark of virtue on his outward parts. (3.2.81-82)

   _____ : _____
   _____

© Novel Units, Inc.   All rights reserved

Name_____

The Merchant of Venice
Unit Test • Level II
page 5

34. The quality of mercy is not strain'd,
    It droppeth as the gentle rain from heaven...
    And that same prayer doth teach us all to render
    The deeds of mercy. (4.1.183...201)

    _____:_____
    _____

35. You take my house when you do take the prop
    That doth sustain my house; you take my life
    When you do take the means whereby I live. (4.1.374-376)

    _____:_____
    _____

Short Answer
Answer each question below in two or three sentences.

36. Compare what happens to Leah's ring to what happens to Portia's and Nerissa's rings.

37. Describe three losses in *The Merchant of Venice*.

38. Compare Portia's reasons for disguising herself as a man with Jessica's reasons.

39. How does Portia honor her dead father?

40. What do you think is the most famous quote from *The Merchant of Venice*—and what does it mean?

Name_____

The Merchant of Venice
Unit Test • Level II
page 6

41. Why does Shylock feel so negatively toward Antonio?

42. How do Shylock and Portia differ in their attitudes about mercy?

43. What are your impressions of Gratiano's personality—and what modern-day actor do you think would make a good Gratiano?

44. Compare Jessica's and Shylock's reasons for converting to Christianity.

45. How does Portia demonstrate her generosity in the play?

46. How does Portia show herself to be an intelligent problem-solver?

47. What does Shylock lose as a result of trying to get Antonio to honor the bond?

48. What is your favorite moment in the play and how does it make you feel?

49. What is one thing you learned from the play about Shakespeare's time—something that you didn't know before?

50. What is one question the play raised in your mind?

Name_____   *The Merchant of Venice*
                                      Unit Test • Level II
                                      page 7

Essay

Directions

After circling your choices (A or B), write your THREE essays on a separate sheet of paper. Your essays should demonstrate that you have read and thought about the play. Credit will be given for organization, coherence, accuracy, and creativity.

I. Analysis (Choose A or B.)

A. Explain why the two central Jewish characters in the story—Shylock and Jessica—convert to Christianity. Describe what Shakespeare's attitude toward these conversions seems to be.
B. Compare and contrast Portia's romance with Jessica's.

II. Evaluation (Choose A or B.)

A. In a recent survey, it was shown that many teachers feel that *The Merchant of Venice* should be taught—but do not teach it. Explain whether or not you feel that the play should be part of the curriculum—and why you, personally, would or would not teach it.
B. Agree or disagree with this statement about the play:
"Shakespeare was not ahead of his time with respect to anti-Semitism; *The Merchant of Venice* shows the playwright to be as anti-Semitic as most Elizabethans of his day."

III. Creative Writing (Choose A or B.)

A. You are Portia. On the evening of your wedding day you sit down to write a letter to your late father, telling him how his "suitor test" has worked out and describing his new son-in-law.
B. You are Shylock. Write a journal entry about recent disappointments in your life. Mention both Jessica and your loss in court. Include your thoughts about mercy, justice, and revenge.

© Novel Units, Inc.   All rights reserved

Answer Key

Activities #1 and #2: There are no right or wrong answers to these and other open-ended activities. Allow students to share their answers with a partner, a small group, or the whole group.

Study Questions

Act I, Scene I
1. Antonio's friends assume his depression stems from worry about his merchant ships.
2. He seems to have a presentiment and says he is simply depressed.
3. Don't act melancholy just to seem wise.
4. He wants to clear his debts so that he can marry Portia.
5. Antonio's wealth is tied up in his ships.

Act I, Scene II
1. Her father has devised a "test" her suitors must pass.
2. Suitors must choose among three chests—gold, silver, and lead; the one who chooses the correct one can ask for Portia's hand.
3. All he talks about is his horse.
4. He is grumpy.
5. He has the combined faults of many men: he frowns, talks about his horses, prances.
6. He can't converse with her as he speaks neither Italian nor French.
7. He is in debt.
8. She likes him neither when he is drunk nor sober.
9. Nerissa favors Bassanio.
10. She says he has the "complexion of a devil" and she would rather give her confession to him than marry him.

Act I, Scene III
1. Bassanio borrows 3,000 ducats for three months.
2. Antonio signs for the loan; if the loan is forfeited, Antonio gives Shylock a pound of flesh.
3. Antonio is a good business risk.
4. He will do business with Bassanio, but he won't eat or drink with him.
5. He is responding to Antonio's comment that Antonio doesn't customarily get engaged in moneylending for interest. Shylock points out that the biblical Jacob engaged in interest, of sorts, by figuring out a way to work a contract he had signed with his uncle, Laban, to his own advantage. He made sure that most of the lambs turned out to be streaked—and hence, went to him.
6. Antonio has spat upon Shylock and denounced his race because Shylock charged high interests on his loans.
7. No, Antonio says that he is just as likely to treat Shylock that way again; Shylock should consider the loan as one to an enemy, not a friend.
8. No, Bassanio protests against the "pound of flesh" clause and urges his friend not to seal such a bond.
9. Shylock has agreed to help Bassanio; Antonio is saying that maybe Shylock isn't so bad after all.

Act II, Scene I
1. The scene is set at Belmont, Portia's estate.
2. The Prince of Morocco suggests that he and lighter-skinned individuals from the North be cut so that he can prove that his blood is redder (and thus, he is worthier of her than they).
3. Suitors must choose the correct coffer from among three inscribed chests—one gold, one silver, one lead.

Act II, Scene II
1. He is deciding whether or not to leave his master, Shylock.
2. His conscience tells him not to run off.
3. Gobbo is old and blind.
4. Launcelot pretends to be someone else and speculates that Launcelot may be dead.
5. He says he is growing hungry and thin in Shylock's service.
6. He has brought a dish of doves.
7. He is in love with Nerissa, Portia's hand-maid.

Act II, Scene III
1. She is sorry, says that she will miss his good humor.
2. She gives him a letter for Lorenzo.
3. She plans to marry Lorenzo.
4. She is Shylock's daughter and a Jew by blood, but she is renouncing her Jewishness in favor of Christianity.

Act II, Scene IV
1. Shylock is invited to dine at Bassanio's.
2. He is paying Launcelot for delivering the letter from Jessica.
3. Lorenzo arranges to meet Gratiano, Salerio, and Solanio at Gratiano's.
4. In it, she directs how he is to come and get her and what she will take from her father's.

Act II, Scene V
1. Shylock is going to dinner at Bassanio's.
2. He goes to feed his hatred, to get revenge.
3. Shylock tells Launcelot he shall not have it as easy as he had as Shylock's servant.
4. Launcelot is responding to Shylock's command that he not call out for Jessica; Launcelot is complaining that Shylock expected to do only as he was told.
5. Shylock tells Jessica to lock up the house and not to look at the Christian masquers when they pass by in the street.
6. She is planning to disappear among the masquers when Lorenzo and the others come for her.

Act II, Scene VI
1. They are waiting for Lorenzo.
2. She is disguised as a boy—a page—to hide her elopement.
3. Antonio has come to tell Gratiano to hurry up, the ship is about to sail.

Act II, Scene VII
1. He is supposed to try to pick the correct one before asking her hand in marriage.
2. "Who chooseth me shall gain what many men desire."
3. "Who chooseth me shall get as much as he deserves."
4. "Who chooseth me must give and hazard all he hath."
5. He humbly admits that while he may not deserve Portia, and while he wouldn't take unnecessary risks for personal gain, he certainly desires her.
6. A scroll saying that everything that glitters is not gold.

Act II, Scene VIII
1. Shylock has learned of Jessica's flight and is looking for her.
2. He and Gratiano are on their way to Belmont.
3. They want to tell him what they've heard about the loss of a ship, in case it is his.

Act II, Scene IX
1. They have to promise that they will leave immediately and pursue Portia no longer if they fail the test.
2. He chooses the silver one because he arrogantly assumes he deserves Portia.
3. Bassanio has arrived.

Act III, Scene I
1. The ship wrecked was Antonio's.
2. He is in a rage about her departure—and her theft of his money and jewels.
3. He expects Antonio to meet the terms of the bond—to give up a pound of flesh, now that his ships are lost.
4. This is Shylock's response to Salerio's statements that surely Shylock would not actually take Antonio's flesh. Shylock is saying that he is as human as any Christian; he has been wronged by a Christian and he deserves revenge.
5. Tubal has been out looking for Jessica.
6. She has taken jewels from him—including a ring that had been Leah's.
7. Presumably Shylock wants to plan his revenge on Antonio.

Act III, Scene II
1. She wants to enjoy him and put off the moment when she might lose him.
2. If Bassanio makes the wrong choice, Portia suggests it would be better to make a dramatic, swan-like end—to music.
3. Why do people fall in love?
4. He argues that evil and cowardice are often gilded as goodness.
5. He chooses lead because it is the least showy and contains no inscription with false promise—but holds a threat, instead. He finds inside a picture of Portia.
6. Such a loss would foresee the end of her love; she would cry out against him.
7. This gives him easier access to the woman he loves—Portia's maid.
8. Gratiano teasingly refers to her as an "infidel."
9. The letter contains news of Antonio's losses.
10. She offers to repay the debt two or three times over.
11. From what she has heard, he will settle for nothing less than revenge; he will be hard on Antonio.
12. She tells him she wants him to take care of this messy business with Shylock so that they can relax and enjoy each other.

Act III, Scene III
1. He knows that Shylock wants revenge for all the times Antonio took away business by giving interest-free loans.
2. He thinks a decision in his favor would compromise Venice's reputation for justice.

Act III, Scene IV
1. He is Bassanio's friend; he must be a good man like Bassanio.
2. She tells him to take care of the house until Bassanio returns.
3. She says that she and Nerissa will be living in prayer.
4. Bellario is Portia's "cousin"—a lawyer.
5. She tells him to bring to the ferry whatever papers and garments Bellario gives him for her.
6. She tells her hand-maid that they will turn themselves into men.

Act III, Scene V
1. He reminds her that according to the Bible, the sins of the fathers are visited on their children.
2. She will be saved by converting to his faith—Christianity.
3. Apparently Launcelot has fathered the child.
4. He wants to listen to Jessica praise him.

Act IV, Scene I
1. The Duke considers Shylock an "inhuman wretch."
2. He is encouraging Shylock to give a gentlemanly response.
3. Shylock refuses to turn down the Duke's suggestion that he forgive a portion of the loan.
4. He is explaining that he chooses the flesh over money simply because he wants to and compares his dislike of Antonio to many people's apparently groundless dislikes of other things: they just don't happen to like these things.

5. They are pretending to be a lawyer and clerk of the court.
6. Gratiano engages in this name-calling.
7. She is making a plea for Shylock to show mercy—before she starts "playing hardball."
8. He says that wasn't specified in the bond; he probably hopes that Antonio will die.
9. Antonio resigns himself quickly to his fate.
10. They both say they would give up their wives.
11. She points out that it is illegal for a Jew to conspire against the life of a citizen; also the bond says nothing about spilling blood.
12. He must convert to Christianity and half of his money goes to the state—the other half goes to Lorenzo and Jessica on Shylock's death.
13. The Duke spares Shylock's life.
14. The conversion and inheritance are Antonio's ideas.
15. She requests Bassanio's ring.

Act IV, Scene II

1. This is the deed of gift for Lorenzo and Jessica.
2. Nerissa (in disguise) demands it in payment.

Act V, Scene I

1. The messenger announces that Portia will be at Belmont by daybreak. Launcelot announces that Bassanio will be back by morning.
2. They hear music.
3. She wants the servants to say nothing about her absence.
4. They start arguing over the missing ring.
5. They explain what they consider the truth—that the lawyer and clerk demanded the rings as payment.
6. Portia and Nerissa produce the rings, teasing about the "men" they bedded, from whom they retrieved the rings.
7. Three of his ships have returned safely.
8. Portia gives them the deed entitling them to Shylock's property.

Activity #3: I. 1-livery; 2-argosies; 3-bated; 4-infidel; 5-surfeit; 6-rasher; 7-adieu; 8-rheum
II. 1-rheum; 2-infidel; 3-livery; 4-adieu; 5-rasher; 6-bated; 7-argosies; 8-surfeit
III. (Sample answers) 1.a) Prince of Morocco to Portia b) Don't hold my (dark) skin color against me. c) The prince is trying to woo Portia. 2. a)Salerio to Antonio b)You are distressed about your ships. c)Salerio is trying to figure out why Antonio is blue. 3. a)Antonio to Solanio b) I'm so upset, I'll hardly have a pound of flesh to give Shylock. c)Knowing that he must forfeit on the loan, Antonio is predicting that Shylock will demand his flesh. 4. a)Gratiano to Lorenzo and Jessica b)Who's that? Lorenzo and his non-Christian girlfriend. c) Gratiano is teasing about Jessica's Jewishness. 5. a) Nerissa to Portia b) Those with too much are as bad off as those who have too little. c) Nerissa is chiding well-off Portia for wallowing in misery. 6. a) Launcelot to Jessica b)If more Jews convert, as you are, the price of pigs will go up c) Launcelot doesn't entirely approve of Jessica's converting in order to marry Lorenzo. 7. a) Launcelot to Jessica b) Good-bye, I know that a Christian—Lorenzo—has won you. c) Launcelot is leaving Shylock's employ and, having agreed to deliver a letter to Lorenzo, indicates he knows about their impending elopement. 8. a) Shylock to Antonio b) You come asking for money after spitting on me. c) Shylock is responding to his old enemy's request for a loan.

Activity #4: 1-a; 2-c; 3-d; 4-b; 5-a; 6-b; 7-c
Activity #5: 1-a; 2-a: 3-b; 4-b; 5-a
Activity #6: I. 1-g;2-k;3-h;4-c;5-m;6-d;7-p;8-b;9-j;10-q;11-e;12-o;13-n;14-a;15-l;16-i;17-f
(Sentences will vary.)

Activity #7: Individual response.

Activity #8: A. Mrs. Malaprop was a character in Sheridan's The Rivals (1775), noted for her misapplication of words.
B. 1-affection; 2-signify; 3-pertinent; 4-effect; 5-inhibit; 6-approach; 7-cogitation
C. Answers will vary (e.g., Homer Simpson, Archie Bunker, Kramer)

Activity #9: A. 1-Gratiano a) dam-block b) damn-oath; 2-Portia a) most good b) animal; 3-Lorenzo a) gentle b) gentile-non-Jew; 4-Jessica a) immodest b) illuminated; 5-Salerio a) fleece—sheep's wool b) fleets-ships; B and C: Answers will vary.

Activity #10: Answers will vary.
a-Phoebus-sun god; b-Hercules-strong hero;Lichas-herald who delivered poisoned robe to Hercules and turned to stone; Alcides-Hercules; c-Hagar-mother of Ishmael; d-Troy-ancient Greek city; Dardanian wives-Trojan wives (of soldiers in the war between Greeks and Trojans); e-Jason-hero, leader of the Argonauts; f-Scylla and Charybdis—sea monsters, one of which captured victims which the other missed; g-Daniel-biblical hero who secured justice for Susannah; h-Barabbas-thief freed by Pilate when Jesus was crucified and also the name of Marlowe's villain in *The Jew of Malta*; i-Troilus and Cressid (Chaucer) faithful and faithless lovers; j-Thisbe-heroine of Ovid's tragedy; k-Dido-Queen of Carthage, loved and abandoned by Aeneas; l-Medea -sorceress who helped Jason and and Aeson—Jason's father, restored to youth by Medea

Activities #11 and #12: Answers will vary.

Activity #13: Crossword solution is on last page

Comprehension Quiz, Level I
True/False: 1-T; 2-F; 3-F; 4-T; 5-F; 6-T; 7-F; 8-T; 9-F; 10-F; 11-T; 12-T; 13-F; 14-F; 15-F
Matching: 16-c; 17-d; 18-f; 19-h; 20-a

Comprehension Quiz, Level II (Accept approximate answers.)
1-depression; 2-in love with a beautiful, wealthy woman named Portia; 3-debts; 4-ships at sea; 5-maid Nerissa; 6-father; 7-chest; 8-Bassanio; 9-3,000 ducats; 10-three; 11-lent money for free; 12-spat on; 13-a pound of Antonio's flesh; 14-Bassanio
Short Answer: 15-Launcelot has decided to leave his master, Shylock, and work for Bassanio. 16-Launcelot's father, Old Gobbo, is old and blind. 17-Jessica wants to marry Lorenzo, a Christian. 18-Jessica has outlined the arrangements for running away with Lorenzo—when and where they will meet, what they will take from her father's house. 19-She takes gold and jewels to finance her honeymoon. 20-Shylock is enraged about the loss of his daughter—and his money—and goes looking for her.

Unit Test, Level I
Identification: 1-B; 2-D; 3-K; 4-H; 5-G; 6-E; 7-L; 8-N; 9-M; 10-A; 11-I; 12-O; 13-J; 14-F; 15-C
Sequence: 16-c; 17-b; 18-e; 19-a; 20-d
Quotations: 21-d; 22-c; 23-a; 24-a; 25-b; 26-b; 27-d; 28-c; 29-b; 30-c; 31-d; 32-b; 33-d; 34-a; 35-c
Multiple Choice: 36-B; 37-C; 38-A; 39-D; 40-D; 41-B; 42-A; 43-D; 44-C; 45-C; 46-A; 47-B; 48-D; 49-C; 50-B

Unit Test, Level II
Identification: 1-Bassanio; 2-Salerio and Solanio; 3-Old Gobbo; 4-Shylock; 5-Lorenzo; 6-Prince of Morocco; 7-Leonardo; 8-Nerissa; 9-Portia; 10-Antonio; 11-Tubal; 12-Jessica; 13-Launcelot; 14-Aragon; 15-Gratiano

Vocabulary
(Accept equivalent answers): 16-spit; 17-trifling; 18-cheat; 19-merchant ships; 20-scorned;

Quotations
21-Antonio: I'm just destined to be sad; 22-Gratiano: Don't be melancholy just to look wise; 23-Bassanio: To find an arrow I'd lost, I used to fire off another; now I'll try asking you for another loan; 24-Nerissa; Those who have too much can suffer as much as those with too little; 25-Portia: Sometimes you may think about behaving one way, but your emotions take over; 26-Shylock: Antonio is a good business risk, but anything could happen to his ships; 27-Shylock: I will do business with you, but I will not share my private life with you as a friend; 28-Antonio: He can even use the Bible to defend his sinfulness. 29-Shylock: You bad-mouthed me and spat on me; 30-Launcelot: You are wise if you recognize your own son; 31-(words found on the scroll in the gold chest, as read by the Prince of Morocco): Not everything that looks valuable is really valuable; 32-Shylock: Isn't a Jew a human being?; 33-Bassanio: People can hide their evil or cowardice behind seeming goodness; 34-Portia:It is good to show some compassion and forgiveness; 35-Shylock:You might as well kill me. You're taking everything when you take my job and my belongings.

Short Answer
36. All the rings start out as gifts and end up as payments. Jessica steals Leah's ring (presumably Leah is her mother) from her father and trades it for a monkey. Portia and Nerissa give their rings to Bassanio and Gratiano, respectively—and these two give the rings in payment to the "lawyer" and "clerk" who outwit Shylock in court. 37. Sample: Antonio loses his ships and mirth; Shylock loses his daughter and property; Jessica has apparently lost her mother and Shylock, her father. 38. Portia wants to see that her husband's friend, Antonio, isn't forced to give up a pound of flesh for forfeiting on a loan, so she disguises herself as a lawyer. Jessica wants to elope with Lorenzo without her father's knowledge, so she dresses as a boy and joins the group of "masquers" who have come for her. 39. Portia follows through on the three-coffer test her father has devised for her suitors—even though she'd rather not. 40. Answers will vary: Most students will probably pick Shylock's "Hath not a Jew eyes" speech. 41. Shylock wants revenge; Antonio has undercut Shylock's moneylending practice, spat on him, bad-mouthed his race. 42. Portia points out that to be merciful and forgive is virtuous; Shylock is not interested in mercy—but in justice according to the letter of the law, even if that means some people get hurt. 43. He is outgoing, outspoken, flirtatious, witty, sometimes sharp-tongued. Sample responses for suggested actors: Billy Crystal, Bruce Willis, Jerry Seinfeld. 44. Jessica wants to convert—sees Christianity as a route to marriage (Lorenzo) and freedom. Shylock is forced to convert as a condition of the court. 45. When Portia learns that her husband's friend—whom she has never met—owes money, she immediately offers to pay the debt. 46. Portia figures out a way to save Antonio's life—despite the bond he signed—by pointing out a technicality of sorts. The bond promised a pound of Antonio's flesh, but said nothing about giving any blood. Also, as a Jew Shylock is an alien, and Portia emphasizes that for him to plot against the life of a citizen is a crime. 47. Shylock loses his faith (he is forced to convert) and much of his wealth (half of his fortune goes to the state, the other half goes to Lorenzo and Jessica upon Shylock's death. 48-50. Personal response.

Essay: I. A. Students who choose (A) should explain that Shylock's conversion is forced, whereas Jessica's is not. Students might go on to argue either that Shakespeare seems to be saying that Shylock and Jessica will be "saved" by their conversion—as Jessica seems to think—or that Shakespeare is pointing out the cruelty behind the anti-Semitism of his time—that Shylock, whose faith is such an essential part of him—can have that faith torn away, and Jessica would have to renounce her Jewishness in order to marry the one she loves.
B. Students who select (B) might include these points: Portia falls in love with a man who is in debt and who allows his friend to get into a troublesome situation while helping him out. The man Jessica falls in love with allows his fiancee to rob her own father to finance their honeymoon. Both women are involved in a transition from single to married status—but it is Jessica who undergoes the more fundamental transformation (changing not only in her status as Shylock's daughter, but losing her Jewishness). Portia's dead father would no doubt approve of her choice—and her romance seems

fully supported by the Christian/wealthy/Venetian society of which she is a member, whereas it is not clear that Jessica—even as Lorenzo's wife—will ever be fully accepted into this society.

II. A. Students who choose (A) might support the point of view of those teachers who feel that the play's literary value does not counterbalance its rabid anti-Semitism. Or they might maintain that while the play actually highlights—and attacks—the anti-Semitism of Elizabethan times, Shakespeare's ironies might be lost on many students, who will accept and even laugh at the Jewish stereotype instead of seeing it for what it is. On the other hand, teachers might defend teaching the play either by maintaining that it is not primarily about Jewishness at all, in any case, but about issues of commitment and loss. Or teachers might defend the play's place in the curriculum by stating that regardless of Shakespeare's personal attitudes toward Jews, the play teaches students about an historical reality during the Elizabethan period—while offering an interesting, tragicomical story.

B. Students who choose (B) should begin by outlining the status of Jews in Elizabethan England—Jews had been cast out of England 300 years before the play was written; of the few that remained during Shakespeare's time, one of the only jobs they were allowed by law was moneylending. Numerous myths about Jews (such as their propensity for the blood of Christian children) survived in varying forms. The essay should focus on the Jewish characters—primarily Shylock and Jessica—and examine some of these questions. Is Shylock's "Hath not a Jew eyes" speech a poignant attack on anti-Semitism? Or does his subsequent behavior show that he is simply a good talker—an eloquent villain? Is he deeply hurt by the loss of his daughter—or more concerned about the loss of his money and jewels? Does he miss Leah's ring for the memories it holds—or the monetary value? Is Shakespeare reminding us that the only legitimate job a Jew could have was moneylender and that it was Elizabethan society that forced Shylock into this position—or is he simply portraying yet another character who fits the stereotype of the miserly, money-grubbing Jew?

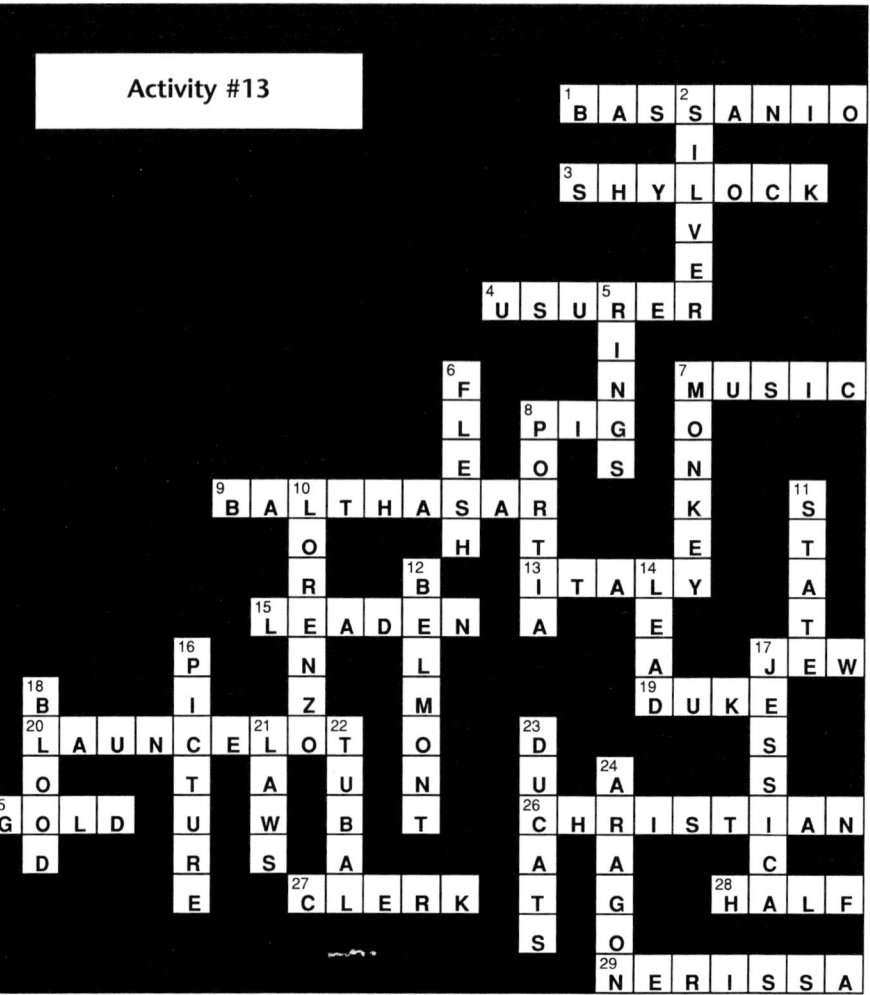

© Novel Units, Inc.   All rights reserved